COMPUTERS AND ROBOTS

Computers are more than just calculators.

What is a computer?

For many years, scientists and engineers worked to make a machine that could calculate numbers quickly and efficiently. The machine they invented is called a computer.

A computer is different from an ordinary calculator, because it has a memory that can store a large amount of information.

Why is a computer useful?

A computer can have huge amounts of information programmed into its memory, much more than any person can remember. Computers are, therefore, very useful not only for work but also for fun, such as computer games.

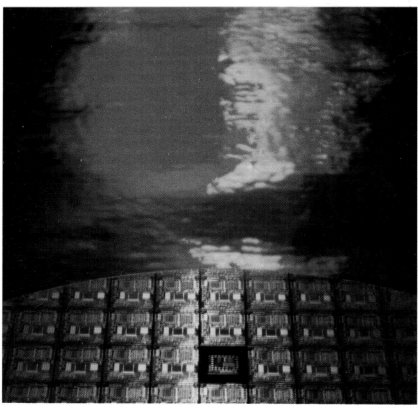

Technology has advanced with the use of microchips.

What is a computer program?

A computer cannot use information or do calculations unless it contains a program. A computer program is made up of instructions

that are put into the main memory of the computer by a computer programmer. There are many sorts of programs, such as those that make words and pictures or music. Extremely complicated programs are used to organise a country's defence forces.

A game program makes using a computer fun.

What is computer language?

In order that computer programs can be used all over the world, special codes, or languages, have been invented.
There are several different languages, such as Basic, Pascal, 'C', and Cobol.
Every program is written in computer language.

What is hardware and software?

'Hardware' is the name given to the computer itself. It also includes all the equipment necessary to make it work, such as the discs, the keyboard and the screen.

'Software' is the name given to the programs which are contained in the discs. Hardware, therefore, are the hard parts of the machine which you can see, software is not visible.

The electronic components of a computer are hard

Computer equipment

screen or monitor

keyboard

printer

scanner

mouse and joystick

Who invented the computer?

An English professor of mathematics called Charles Babbage (1792-1871) first had the idea of a calculating machine. However, he never saw his idea become reality because the technology of his time was not advanced enough to enable him to build it. The notes he made were useful for other inventors.

Charles Babbage.

What is an abacus?

An abacus is a simple calculating machine. By moving the beads along the rods it is possible to add, subtract, multiply and divide.

The abacus has been used for centuries in many parts of the world. It is the predecessor of the calculator and the computer. The abacus is still used today in some Far Eastern countries, by bankers, mathematicians and astronomers.

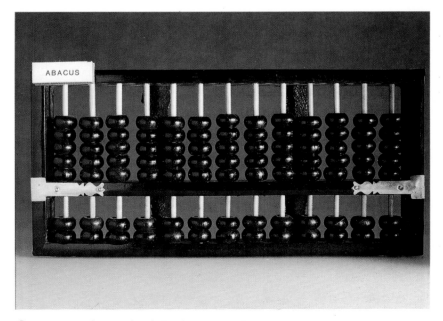

Sums can be calculated on an abacus.

How big was the first computer?

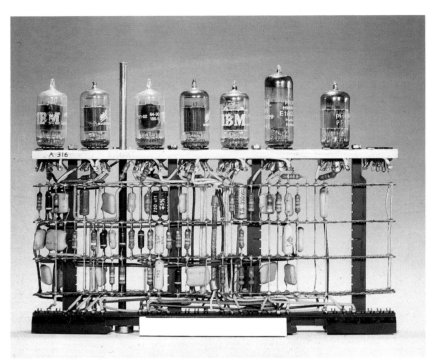
The first computers used valves.

The first electronic computer was built in 1945 by the United States Army. The computer was 30 metres long, 3 metres high and 1 metre wide. It weighed 30 tonnes and was equipped with 18,000 radio valves. Unfortunately, the heat given out by the computer was so hot that the valves often burnt out.

Why do computers need power?

No machine can work without a power source. The computer is powered by electricity.
There are also smaller, portable computers which are powered by batteries. Portable computers enable business men and women to work whilst they are travelling by aeroplane or train.

A portable computer runs on batteries.

What is a robot?

A robot is a mechanical invention designed to imitate human actions. Robots in science fiction films are often made to look like people, too. A robot uses photo-electric cells to 'see', it 'hears' with micro-phones, and 'feels' with thermometers. Robots can be programmed to carry out a variety of tasks.

This robot has been programmed to play the guitar.

How does a computer remember?

Computers have two types of memory: a permanent one, ROM (Read Only Memory) and RAM (Random Access Memory). RAM is the memory into which pro-grams and information are loaded.

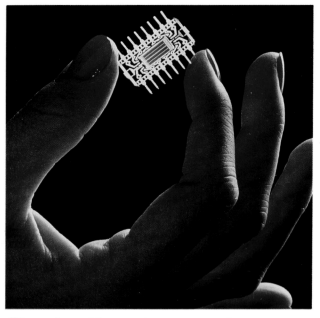

The microchip can be seen at the centre.

What is a microchip?

A microchip is a tiny square of silicon containing tiny electronic circuits which enable electricity to pass through.

A computer contains many microchips which perform different functions. Some chips, called 'microprocessors' are themselves mini computers.

How are microchips protected?

Microchips are very sensitive to dirt. Even the tiniest specks of dust and dirt can prevent them from working properly.

That is why microchips are contained in a protective package. The microchip is connected to the rest of the computer, or whatever machine it is in, by little 'pins'. These pins allow connections to be made to each part of the computer.

A microchip is contained inside a protective package.

How does a computer work?

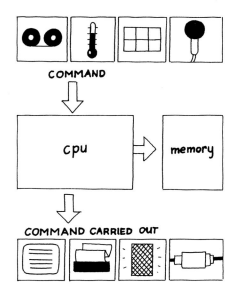

COMMAND

cpu → memory

COMMAND CARRIED OUT

When a person enters a command into a computer, it checks that there is a program available to answer the command. That program is transferred from the hard disc (the permanent memory) to the RAM memory.

A computer is a complex machine.

Next, the CPU (Central Processing Unit) works on the new information. The CPU takes the new information and, using the instructions in the program, performs a calculation. The result is stored in the RAM memory. When the result is needed, the CPU sends it to the screen or the printer.

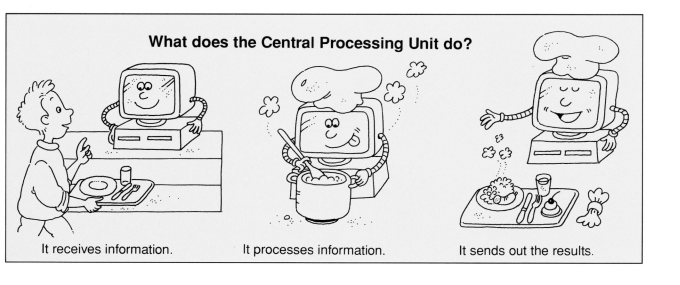

What does the Central Processing Unit do?

It receives information.　　It processes information.　　It sends out the results.

Are computer games educational?

A large number of computerised games and toys are available. Some are very simple and others are extremely complicated. There are games of skill, for example,

and games which concentrate on speed and reaction.
Every game teaches something.
It is not a good idea to spend too much time playing games on the computer, however, as your friends and schoolwork will get forgotten.

Just one of many computer games.

What is a monitor?

A monitor looks like a small television screen. When a disc is put into the computer, the operator calls up the information from the disc and it is shown on the screen. Screens used to be black and white only, but now they can also be in colour.

Can computers help pilots learn to fly?

Trainee pilots do not learn to fly in real aeroplanes – it would be dangerous. They learn in a flight simulator. This looks like a cockpit, but all the dials and buttons are linked to a computer.

The computer shows how the aeroplane would fly if the pilot were in the air.

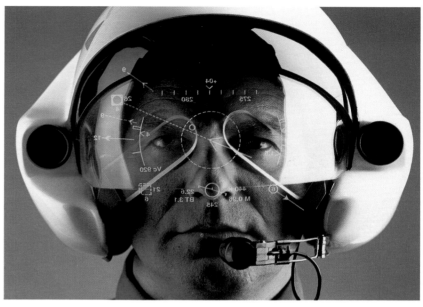

Instructions are projected on to the pilot's visor.

What is CAD?

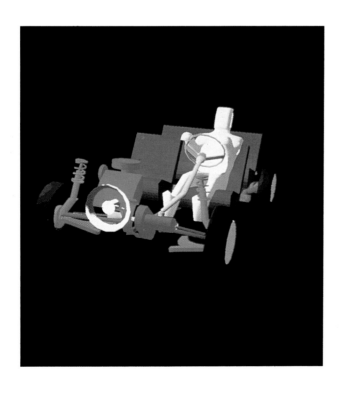

CAD (Computer Aided Design) is a program used by engineers who design new cars, for example. The engineer puts his plans and drawings into the computer which shows them on the screen from every angle. This allows the engineer to check his design.

The CAD shows how a design will look.

How are computers used in banks?

Banks use computers for many jobs.

Computers are used in every bank. One job that a computer does is to calculate the amount of money withdrawn and deposited in the bank each day. Many banks also have automatic cash dispensers. A customer puts a special card, stamped with a set of figures, into the dispenser. The customer taps in a code number and the computer matches it with the number on the card. Then it gives the amount of money that the customer has asked for.

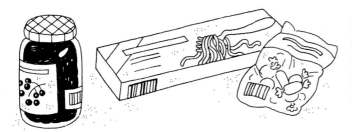

What are bar codes?

On packs of food, newspapers and books you will often see a group of black lines. This is called a bar code. When a customer buys an item, the shop assistant passes the bar code under a special computer which 'reads' it and calls up the correct price.

Many items in shops have bar codes.

Step by step

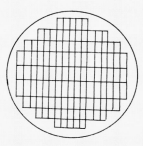

The microchips are designed on large panels.

They are reduced photographically on to a thin disc of silicon (the wafer).

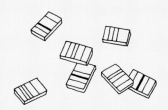

The wafer is cut into hundreds of microchips.

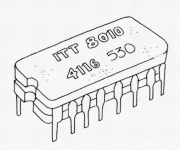

Each microchip is protected inside a cover.

How are microchips made?

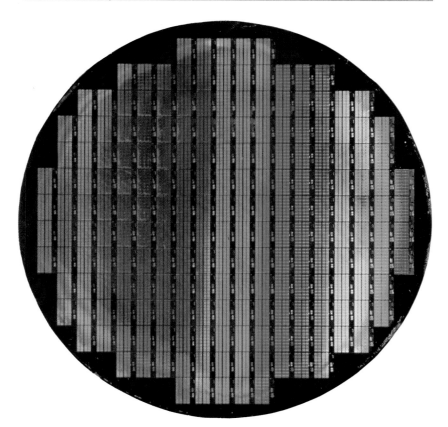

Microchips on a silicon wafer.

Microchips are made up as part of a silicon disc called a wafer. The wafer is about 10 to 15 cm across.

First, the chips are designed, then they are reproduced photographically on the silicon. Finally, the chips are cut out. Hundreds of chips can be made from one wafer.

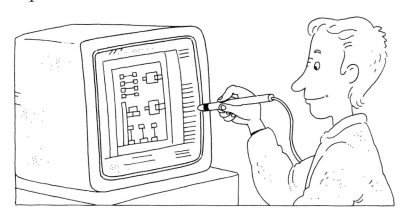

What is a mouse?

stop the cursor, he presses the button on the box.

A mouse makes the cursor move.

A mouse is a small box with a button on top which is used to give instructions to the computer. When the mouse is moved around a flat surface it makes the cursor move about the screen. When the operator wants to

What is LOGO?

LOGO is a simple program, used in children's games. It asks questions so that the operator can decide on the next move to make. For example, a picture of an animal appears on the screen to ask questions. When the operator wants to draw a line, the animal asks, 'How many steps do you want to take?' The answer will decide how long the line is.

Are all computers fast?

The main advantage of computers is that they can do calculations very quickly.
Some computers can perform millions of calculations per

Computers are designed to work quickly.

second. Of course such computers are very expensive. Even a personal computer can make one million calculations every second!

What is a computer virus?

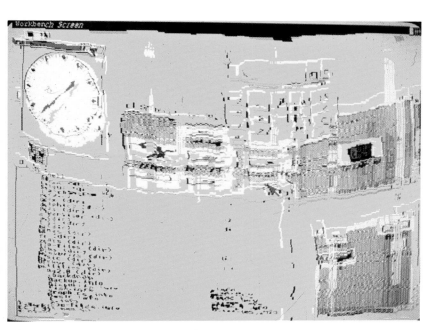

A program is ruined by a virus.

A virus is a program that can spoil another program when it comes into contact with it. The virus spreads from one disc to another when the discs are copied.
Viruses can destroy a valuable program and spoil all the work that has been done.

How does a computer calculate?

A computer, recognises only two figures, 1 and 0. It uses 1 and 0 to do all its calculations. This is called the binary system.

When the computer calculates, electric pulses race through a maze of circuit breakers.

The figure 0 means that a circuit is closed and the electric pulse cannot pass. The figure 1 represents an open circuit and the pulse can go through. 0 and 1 are used in many combinations to make up the letters of the alphabet.

Computers use only two digits to make letters and figures.

The computer alphabet

A = 110001	H = 111000	O = 100110	U = 010100
B = 110010	I = 111001	P = 100111	V = 010101
C = 110011	J = 100001	Q = 101000	W = 010110
D = 110100	K = 100010	R = 101001	X = 010111
E = 110101	L = 100011	S = 010010	Y = 011000
F = 110110	M = 100100	T = 010011	Z = 011001
G = 110111	N = 100101		

How does a robot receive orders?

Computers are used to give instructions to robots. Some robots are guided from a distance, while others contain a computer inside them. In either case, a computer program controls the robot.

Robots can also be toys.

What is an in-flight computer?

In-flight computers are built into aeroplanes. Useful information, such as the direction of the wind and the aeroplane's height, is stored and used by the computer to make sure that the aeroplane is flying on the safest course.

A computer used in a car.

What is a printer?

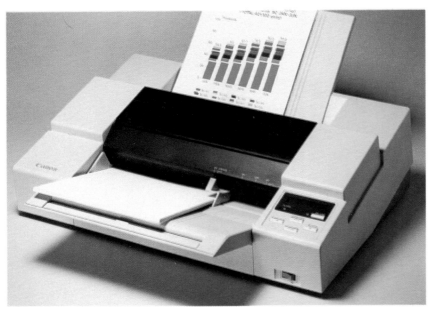

A printer is the machine used to transfer information from a computer on to paper. There are many different types of printer. Some print with ribbons, like typewriters, but the most modern printers use lasers. These are extremely fast and silent when they print.

Some modern printers can print in colour.

What is a scanner?

A scanner is a machine which turns objects or drawings into information that can be stored in a computer. The scanner is passed over pictures and the information is stored in the computer's memory. The information can be called up on the screen and used or changed.

Scanners are often used in hospitals.

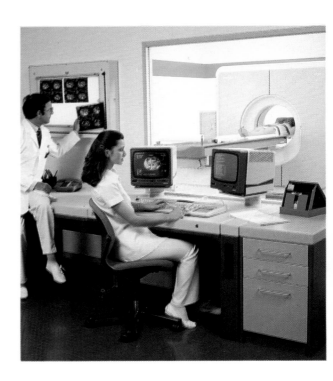

Can robots replace people?

Robots are better workers than people in some ways. For example, although they may break down, they are never ill. They can work day and night without stopping and they do not need holidays.

Robots can be used, therefore, to replace people in jobs that are repetitive and boring. Robots will never replace humans, because they need humans to program and guide them.

A robot does not stop working.

20

Finding out what a computer can do.

What is computer science?

Computer science is the understanding of computers and how they work. Computers play an important part in our lives so it is a good idea to try to understand something about

them. Try to use a computer at home or at school and understand what they can do.

Can computers be used for teaching?

Computers can be used to learn from at school and at home. There are many programs to learn from, such as spelling, history and maths.
These teaching programs show the operator his mistakes and tell him when the answers are correct.

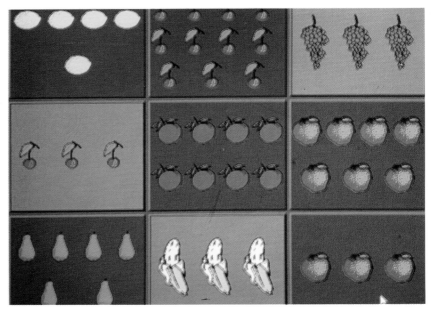

Children can learn to count on a computer.

Which machines use a microchip?

Microchips are not only to be found in computers, they are also used in many different machines: televisions, video recorders, sewing machines, washing machines, cars, cameras ... the list is endless.
Our everyday life is made much easier by this tiny device.

Microchips are used in some toys.

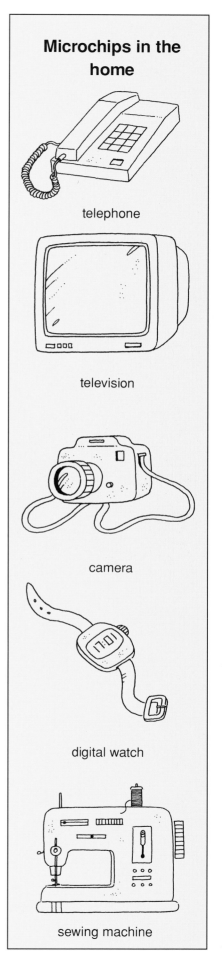

Microchips in the home

telephone

television

camera

digital watch

sewing machine

How is a microchip checked for mistakes?

Checking the microchips on a silicon wafer.

Microchips hold lots of information and mistakes can occur when they are being made. So they are checked while they are still on the silicon wafer.
Tiny wires, or filaments, transmit the information in the microchips to a computer for checking.

2 BITS

1 BYTE

What are bits and bytes?

A bit is one of two figures, 0 or 1, in the binary system – which the computer uses to perform calculations.
A byte is a group of eight bits. These eight bits are used to make 256 different combinations, each one representing a letter, a number, or a symbol.

Is a robot intelligent?

A robot can work for hours underwater. It can see in the dark or calculate difficult sums. But it can only do what it has been told to do by a programmer. A robot cannot think for itself or use common sense. So it has no intelligence.

A robot to stir your drink?

Can computers be linked up to each other?

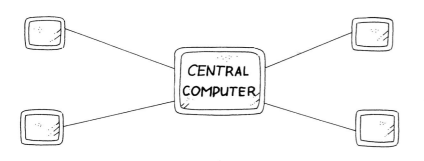

CENTRAL COMPUTER

Large businesses often have a central computer that stores all the information to do with the company. This central computer is linked to other, smaller computers, known as terminals, in separate offices. Operators using the terminals can draw information from the main computer. When they have used the information, they return it to the central computer where it is stored.

A central computer stores a company's information.

Can computers talk?

Some microchips understand words and imitate the human voice. These microchips are found in video games and in the big computers used by banks. A bank's computer can give customers information about their accounts over the telephone.

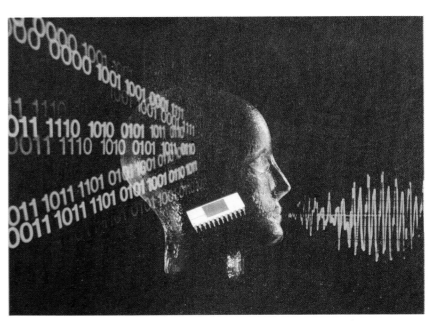

Computers can imitate the human voice.

Can computers hear?

It is far more complicated for a computer to hear than to speak. Each person's voice is different and there are many ways of saying the same thing. However, there are 'listening' microchips, which are programmed to recognise one voice only.

This lamp can obey spoken commands.

How is information stored in a computer?

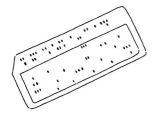

perforated card

cassette

floppy disc

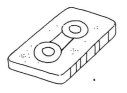

CD-ROM

Information used to be stored on perforated cards (cards with holes in them). However, these cards could not hold much information, and they were replaced by magnetic tapes, and then by floppy discs. Nowadays information may also be stored on electronic discs (CD-ROM) which use lasers.

CD-ROM discs contain a huge amount of information.

What is a hard disc?

A hard disc is the permanent memory stored in the computer. It contains important programs and information.

What is a floppy disc?

A floppy disc can be taken in and out of the computer. Programs and information can be stored on this type of disc, too.

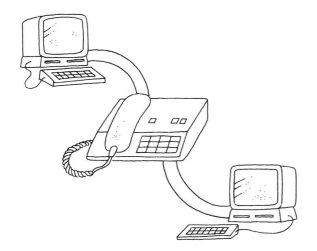

What is a modem?

A modem is a machine which transforms computer signals so that information can be sent from one computer to another using telephone lines.

Can computers play chess?

Chess can be played on a computer chessboard.

It is possible to have a game of chess with a computer by playing on an electronic chessboard, or by loading the computer with the correct game program.

A computer can calculate very quickly and remember what it has done, so it is difficult to beat. There are several degrees of difficulty that you can play. At the easiest level the computer is programmed so that it allows you extra time to think about your next move.

Can a computer draw?

A computer cannot draw by itself. It has no imagination, but there are programs which allow the operator to make the computer draw. The operator uses a mouse to draw lines. Each drawing can be copied. Surfaces can be shaded and coloured at the touch of a button. Drawings can be made larger or smaller.

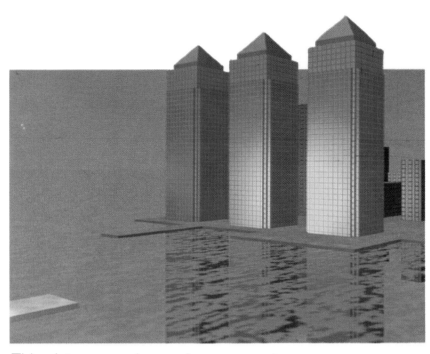

This picture was done using a computer.

Can a computer make music?

A computer can copy the sounds made by different musical instruments. The special programs for this contain microchips that are able to produce sounds. The keyboard for making music on a computer looks like the keyboard of a piano.

A synthesizer uses a computer.

What does automation mean?

A robot is instructed to perform certain actions.

Automation is the word given for the way machines are programmed to work automatically.
Many industries use automatic machines. For example, automated paint spraying is used in car factories.

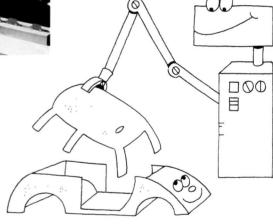

Computers direct robots which carry out orders exactly. Automation means that machines can do certain tasks more quickly and efficiently than people.

What do Kb and Mb mean?

Kb (Kilobytes) and Mb (Megabytes) show the capacity of the memory of a microchip or a floppy disc. A disc of 720 Kb, for example, can store about 720,000 letters, figures or symbols.

Not all computers are as complex as this.

How the computer helps ...

the shopkeeper

It checks the quantities of stock sold or left in the shop.

the doctor

It stores information about each patient.

the garage owner

It checks the customers' accounts.

the nursery gardener

It controls the temperature in the greenhouses.

Who uses a computer?

Nowadays computers are used in most offices. They are sometimes used in the home for playing games.

Many people have a PC (personal computer) that they use to write letters or stories on, or to store useful information, such as recipes or shopping lists.

Many different sorts of people use computers in their work: shopkeepers, doctors, garage owners, nursery gardeners.

The computer control centre of a large company.

Can a computer be artistic?

Although a computer cannot make sculptures or carve wood or stone, it can be used to create pictures and compose music.

In the future, computers will be programmed to do these jobs better but it is unlikely that they will replace human artists.

A drawing on a computer screen.

Can a computer make mistakes?

Part of a robot's arm.

No, a computer cannot make mistakes, it can only follow orders.

If a mistake is found it must have been made by the computer programmer when he, or she, was writing the instructions in the program.

If there is a mistake in the program the computer will not function correctly.

What is artificial intelligence?

People have often wondered if it would be possible to build a machine that is able to think.

This sort of machine would not need a programmer to give it orders, but would be able to make decisions by itself. To do this, the computer would have to be able to learn by itself. Then the machine could be said to have artificial intelligence.

The human brain is like a computer.

What are hackers?

Some computers contain information that is top secret. It is impossible to gain access to this information without knowing a special code. However, certain people, called hackers, use their computers to gain access to the secret information. Hackers do not always do this because they need the information, they do it for the challenge.

Where does the word 'robot' come from?

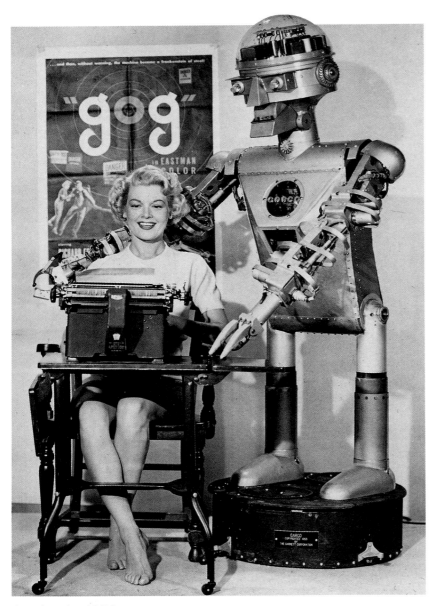

A robot in 1953.

The word 'robot' was first used in 1920 when Karel Capek, a Czechoslovakian man, wrote a play in which people were taken over by automatons that looked like human beings.

Capek called the automatons 'robots', from the Czech word 'robota' which means work.

Since then, the word 'robot' has been used to describe many types of automatic machine.

Robots are mechanical devices that copy the action of human arms and are controlled by computers.

Index

Sources of photographs

Alcatel Bell: 4, 8 b, 9, 15 t, 16, 29; Blaupunkt: 17 b; British Embassy: 28 t, 30 b; Canon: 18 t, 28 b; Chriet Titulaer Productions: 5 b, 6 t, 11 b, 17 t, 21, 23 t, 25, 30 t; Digital: 2 t; Gety: 10, 15 b, 20 b; Hendrikx, I.: 12, 27 b; House of the Future Ltd.: 24 b; IBM: 3, 13; Intel: 2 b; ITT: 31; Nina Aka: 19; Novag Industries: 26; Philips: 14, 20 t, 22, 24 t; Render Star: 27 t; Sextant Avionique: 11 t; Siemens: 8 t, 18 b; Taito: 7; Toshiba: 6 b; Wide World Photo: 32.